To my three designers, Nevae, Kayla, and Romie—
may you always have curious minds
and continue to inspire with your very big hearts

BEACH LANE BOOKS
An imprint of Simon & Schuster Children's Publishing Division
1230 Avenue of the Americas, New York, New York 10020
© 2023 by Aura Lewis
Book design by Sonia Chaghatzbanian © 2023 by Simon & Schuster, Inc.
All rights reserved, including the right of reproduction in whole or in part in any form.
BEACH LANE BOOKS and colophon are trademarks of Simon & Schuster, Inc.
For information about special discounts for bulk purchases, please contact Simon & Schuster Special Sales
at 1-866-506-1949 or business@simonandschuster.com.
The Simon & Schuster Speakers Bureau can bring authors to your live event. For more information
or to book an event, contact the Simon & Schuster Speakers Bureau at 1-866-248-3049
or visit our website at www.simonspeakers.com.
The text for this book was set in Excelsior LT Std.
The illustrations for this book were rendered in mixed media.
Manufactured in China
0323 SCP
First Edition
10 9 8 7 6 5 4 3 2 1
CIP data for this book is available from the Library of Congress.
ISBN 9781665904452
ISBN 9781665904469 (ebook)

A CURIOUS MIND and a Very Big Heart

The Story of Designer and Innovator Sara Little Turnbull

written and illustrated by
AURA LEWIS

Beach Lane Books • New York London Toronto Sydney New Delhi

Sara Little was a most curious child.
Small as a button, she had a big heart,
a huge imagination,
and a million questions about the world.

Why?
What?
How?

Sara especially loved to look at beautiful things.
She often visited museums to see some of her favorites.

And at home Sara and her mother looked carefully
at small things too:

The delicate shape of an egg.
The iridescent skin of a purple onion.
How beautiful and new the world can be
when you look very closely!

When Sara got older, her curiosity and love of beauty led her to study design.

what is design?

Design is...

imagining,

planning

& CREATING

something useful.

People noticed Sara's pizzazz and her keen sense of style.
She was soon hired as the decorating editor at the
magazine *House Beautiful*, where she wrote about
designing homes that looked and felt tip-top.

Sara also became a product designer extraordinaire.

She designed things for herself, like the upside-down clock she wore on her shirt to tell time swiftly and the tucked-away storage spaces in her tiny apartment in New York City.

But mostly Sara loved designing for other people.

Things like ready-to-go ribbons for gifts,

a chewy-gooey cake mix,

good-for-kids sweets,

and light-as-air space suits!

Time and again Sara traveled the world in search of bright ideas. Everywhere she went, she was smitten with the natural beauty she saw, the people she met, and the objects she found.

Sometimes her adventures sparked brand-new designs!

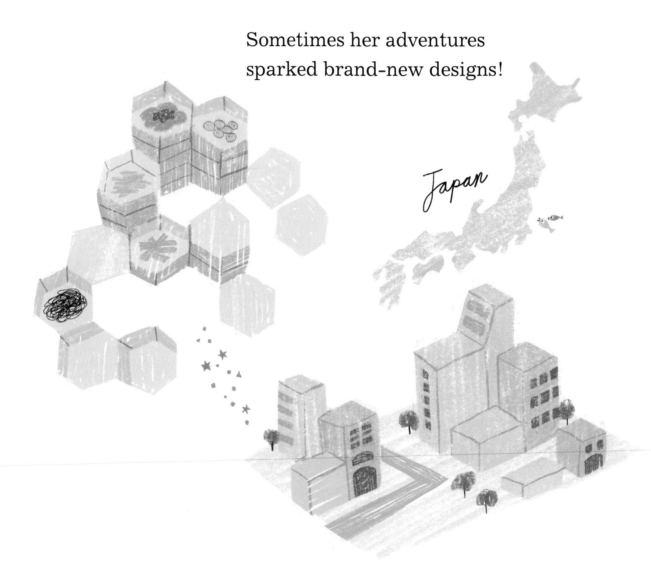

Japan

In Japan, Sara found boxes for pickled vegetables, which made her think of a design for city blocks.

In Malaysia she watched weavers using looms, which helped her design energizing bath towels.

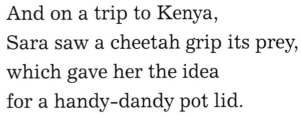

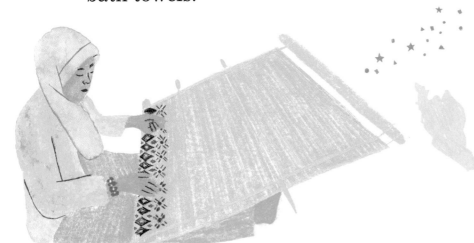

And on a trip to Kenya, Sara saw a cheetah grip its prey, which gave her the idea for a handy-dandy pot lid.

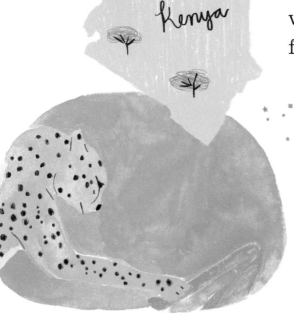

Sara's life was design,

but it wasn't always a piece of cake.

It was often like a tricky puzzle

that was just too hard to solve.

Yet Sara did not put her pencils down
or her ideas away.

She had a big poster in her studio:

If you don't stretch, you don't know where the edge is.

It was a reminder that mistakes can help you grow.

When her sister got sick, Sara sat by her side.
During long days at the hospital,
Sara did what she always did.
She looked carefully at things around her.

Sara noticed that doctors used
particularly cumbersome masks.
They were flat and tough to tie in place.
How could they be better? she wondered.

Then she had a bright idea.

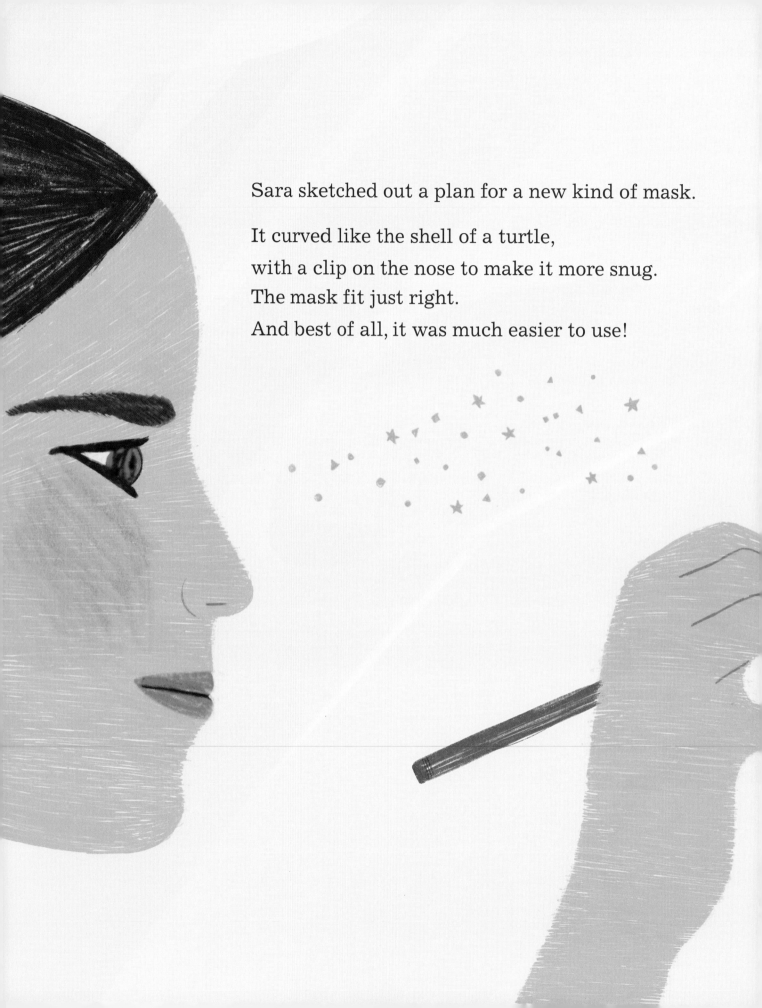

Sara sketched out a plan for a new kind of mask.

It curved like the shell of a turtle,
with a clip on the nose to make it more snug.
The mask fit just right.
And best of all, it was much easier to use!

Sara's design was a smashing success.

It was not perfect,
but with time and with tweaks made by others,
it became the mask that now keeps people safe
all over the world.

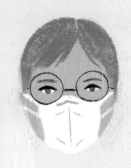

Why?

Why?

Why?

How?

What?

?

And Sara?

She continued to explore and design.
She also became a beloved teacher who inspired
young designers to ask many questions
and see things in a new light.

Design

is

Design is curiosity.

Design is being inventive.

Design is creating order.

More than anything, Sara hoped to make the world
a little bit better with her designs.
And though she was small, she did just that,
with her curious mind and her very big heart.

Magic

More about Sara Little Turnbull

Sara Finkelstein was born on September 21, 1917, in Brooklyn, New York, to a family of Russian Jewish immigrants. She was a bright and precocious child with a big laugh. Sara's mother, who had been educated as a literary scholar in Russia, taught her to look for beauty and design even in small, everyday objects. Sara loved when her mother showed her how to arrange fruit in bowls and how to appreciate the vibrant colors and unique shapes found in nature. Sara also loved visiting museums and went so often that many of the security guards in her favorite museums knew her. She had a tremendous curiosity and later in life said, "I am completely brought up in the tradition to ask questions and be respectful of the fact that most of the answers exist. What you need to do is ask a good question."

In 1935 Sara won a local competition in silk-print design and was awarded a scholarship to attend Parsons School of Design in Manhattan. There she studied advertising design, and after graduating in 1939, she worked as a product designer and art director. She adopted the name Sara Little as her professional title based on her nickname, Little Sara, which was given to her by friends because she was only 4'11" tall.

In 1941 Sara began to write a column titled Girl with a Future for *House Beautiful* magazine. She was eventually hired as decorating editor there, where she made a mark on modern American living and home design. Until that time home entertaining had been a formal affair, and Sara wanted to change that. She introduced her readers to the idea of casual home entertaining, including the concept of a self-serve buffet. Sara later designed informal furniture and tableware as well.

In 1958 Sara founded her own design company, Sara Little Design Consultant, which was a remarkable and trailblazing endeavor for a woman at the time. Shortly after, she wrote an article for *Housewares Review* titled "Forgetting the Little Woman." In it she made the case that too many companies designed products without thinking of their actual consumers. Her article attracted the attention of executives at several large corporations who then hired her as a consultant. Sara went on to advise NASA, Procter & Gamble, General Mills, Coca-Cola, and Volvo (to name just a few!). She became known as "corporate America's secret weapon" for her creative and innovative design solutions, which spanned the gamut from housewares and furniture to toys, medical devices, finger foods, cake mixes, textiles, and space suits.

Though Sara always worked very hard, she also believed that rest was an essential design tool. "I use my resting area whenever I reach a seminal moment in the decision-making process. While resting, I am able to listen to my inner self and explore new directions."

Sara traveled the world widely to learn about and be inspired by how people in different cultures interacted with objects. Among the places she went were Borneo, Jamaica, Malaysia, the Philippines, Kenya, and Japan. On her travels she collected over 3,500 artifacts! "It always starts with a fundamental curiosity. When I can't find the answer in a book, I go out and search for it. The excitement of my life is that I have always jumped into the unknown to find what I needed to know."

One of Sara's most important innovations was the design for a disposable medical mask. In the late 1940s Sara's sister was diagnosed with cancer, and Sara spent many long days with her at the hospital. Watching the doctors and nurses work, she was inspired to create a medical mask that was molded so it would fit better and be easier to use. Initially it was used by construction workers to protect them from inhaling dust. But a few decades later, technology got better, and the mask that Sara had created was enhanced to protect people against germs, too. In 1995 it was developed into the N95 mask that we know today with the same basic features of Sara's design: molded material, a metal nose clip, and elastic straps.

Sometimes Sara tried an idea and it failed. Once, she developed a prototype for flower-shaped medicinal lollipops, but ultimately her idea was rejected for fear that people would overmedicate because the lollipops looked too much like candy. "Ninety percent of my career was made up of failure, but failure is not defeat for those who innovate and look for new horizons."

For twenty years Sara lived in a tiny four-hundred-square-foot room at the Lombardy Hotel in Manhattan. By using collapsible furniture and tucked-away storage spaces, Sara made use of every corner of her apartment. Then, in 1965, she married business executive James Turnbull, and they moved to Washington State. In 1971 Sara founded and directed the Sara Little Center for Design Research at the Tacoma Art Museum in Washington State, which became home to the huge assortment of artifacts that she had collected during her travels, including dishes, vases, dolls, and designer clothes.

Eventually, Sara and James moved to Palo Alto, California, and in 1988 Sara was hired by the Stanford Graduate School of Business. There she established her Process of Change Laboratory for Innovation and Design and became a beloved teacher and mentor to design students from all over the world. She employed a "why-why-why-why-how" technique, where she asked students to explore why people need an object as the path to finding the best design solution. Sara encouraged her students to dig deep to reach the core of a problem, rather than look for superficial solutions. "I see design as essentially creating order, but I also encourage students to learn from their own experience, at times letting their minds meander to discover the unexpected and the creative accident."

Sara felt design was a magical tool that could transform the world and make people's lives better. When she died in 2015, at the age of ninety-seven, she left behind the Sara Little Turnbull Foundation, which awards grants to underrepresented youth and women in design and continues the work of keeping her legacy alive.

Sources and Further Reading

Abdelfatah, Rund, and Ramtin Arablouei. "The Mask." Produced by NPR. *Throughline*, May 14, 2020. Podcast, 41:12. https://www.npr.org/2020/05/13/855405132/the-mask.

"About Sara." Sara Little Turnbull Foundation. Accessed October 23, 2021. https://saralittlefoundation.org/#about-sara-index.

Glaser, Milton, and Steelcase Design Partnership. *Work, Life, Tools: The Things We Use to Do the Things We Do.* New York: Monacelli Press, 1997.

Heller, Steven, and Véronique Vienne, eds. *Citizen Designer: Perspectives on Design Responsibility.* New York: Allworth Press, 2003.

Knight, Heather. "Mother of Invention: High-Energy, Well-Traveled Sara Little Turnbull Teaches Stanford Students How to Build a Better Mousetrap." SFGATE. January 28, 2000. https://www.sfgate.com/bayarea/article/MOTHER-OF -INVENTION-High-energy-well-traveled-2808517.php.

McFadden, Robert D. "Sara Little, Peripatetic Product Designer, Dies at 97." *New York Times*. September 7, 2015. https://www.nytimes.com/2015/09/08/business/sara-little -turnbull-product-designer-inspired-by-anthropology-and-nature-dies-at-97.amp.html.

The New School. "Sara Little Turnbull." Parsons School of Design. Accessed October 23, 2021. https://www.newschool.edu/parsons/profile/sara-little--turnbull/.

Rees, Paula, and Larry Eisenbach. "Ask Why: Sara Little Turnbull." Design Museum Everywhere. April 6, 2020. https://designmuseumfoundation.org/ask-why/.

Turnbull, Sara Little. Interview by Christopher Liechty. Icograda Design Week in Seattle, July 15, 2006. https://youtu.be/4aGRCQplGuE.